Fiona Pitt-Kethley was born in 1954 and studied at the Chelsea School of Art. She is the author of two previous collections of poetry, *Sky Ray Lolly* (1986) and *Private Parts* (1987), and has also written a travel book, *Journeys to the Underworld* (1988). She lives on the Sussex coast, and describes herself as a working poet and a female Casanova.

THE PERFECT MAN

Fiona Pitt-Kethley

AN ABACUS BOOK

Published in Abacus by Sphere Books Ltd 1989

Copyright © Fiona Pitt-Kethley 1989

Printed and bound in Great Britain by
Richard Clay Ltd., Bungay, Suffolk

Sphere Books Ltd
(A division of Orbit House)
Macdonald & Co (Publishers) Ltd
66/73 Shoe Lane, London EC4P 4AB
A member of Maxwell Pergamon Publishing Corporation plc

Contents

Acknowledgements

Some of these poems have been published in *Cosmopolitan*, *London Review of Books*, *The Observer*, *New Statesman and Society*, *The Kentish Companion*, *Bête Noire*, *The Salmon*, *Helikon*, *Review*, *Quarry*, *Verse* and *She*.

Some have been broadcast in a series of *Time For Verse* programmes on Radio 4, others on *Poetry Now*, *Pick of the Week* and *Woman's Hour*.

AIDS was televised on Channel Four's *UK Late*, *Prostitution* was filmed for a Channel Four *Comment*, *That Word* for an edition of *Kilroy* (BBC 1) and *Nothing* was filmed for *Spinsters* – to be shown on Channel Four.

The letters quoted in the notes are private ones apart from those that have been published by *London Review of Books* and *Times Literary Supplement*. The articles included appeared in the *Independent* and *New Statesman*.

The Perfect Man [1]

Fair-haired, blue-eyed, he doesn't swear or drink,
and boasts that he can swim as many lengths
as students he has taught – a lecturer.

He feels I should hand-write my notes to him.
(Word-processed's good enough for all my friends.)
He uses violet ink.

Last week he came to tea and brought me flowers –
the perfect gentleman. He stayed for hours
and hours, not caring that I had to pack –
sort out some clothes and poems for *my work*.
London next morning, Ireland for three days,
(a TV chat show, then a festival.)

The slowness of some academic brains
plants obvious expressions on the face.
He checked the watercolours were all mine,
that I could sing, that I had made the cake . . .
(Was I accomplished enough to be his wife?)
Ah yes, and I had said I'd fixed the roof . . .
My God! I'd rather marry someone's pig.

He talked of Opera. I showed the door
that Jenny Lind had given to our house –
dark oak, heavy and intricately carved.
He looked around, took in the table's mess,
hinted my floppy discs weren't well-maintained,
asked if I 'fed' the bindings on my books.

I gave a parting gift, glad to get rid of them,
four volumes of Sir Walter Scott
to take back to his flat in Camberwell.
(He *would* like Scott.) I hope he feeds them well . . .

[1]Notes on the poems are to be found at the end of the collection.

That Word [2]

'I bet you're glad your daughter wasn't here
tonight to hear *that word*,' I heard one man
say to another man the night I read.
His hair looked dyed. His face was red with rage
which made the bird tattoo flying down his neck
seem extra blue.

I rather wondered if he and his friend
that worded their own daughters at weekends.
Statistics prove lots of men do.

A vicar's girl taught all the class *that word*
when I was nine. I really took to it –
so easy to remember and pronounce
and good for rhymes. It's not a synonym –
an honest word that only means one thing.
I've used it ever since. Beside all that,
I rather like the short, sharp shock it gives
to men with daughters to protect.

Copy Cat

An academic I heard tell's set out
to prove the Bard had a ménage à trois.
His home-computer's stored with word-by-word
analysis of every sonnet line.
He's worked at it for years. What Shakespeare did,
he thinks, he can do too . . .

'The Hidden Persuaders'

I was one of the Oxbridge stream at school.
We were taken off for extra classes,
mainly to groom us for The Interview
and general essays we might have to write.

First, they checked we took the right newspapers
(*Times, Guardian, Daily Telegraph*)
not ones with pieces on randy vicars.
Then, we were handed out a list of books,
all modern, serious but popular,
those that could tell us what we ought to think,
things like Vance Packard's *The Hidden Persuaders*,
The Female Eunuch and *The Naked Ape*.
(I *still* avoid the titles on that list.)
I buggered off, read Jacobean plays –
Beaumont and Fletcher were much more my taste.

I was reminded of a magazine –
'Anne wants to smarten up for her new job'.
Dog's-dinnered generally and blushered-up,
she's stuffed into a yellow suit and heels;
her hair is layered like feathers and highlighted.
Anne says that she is 'pleased with her new look'.
She would – to get away.

We were all studying for A-levels –
three each at least. In my case it was four –
Latin and Greek, Religious Knowledge, Art.
'Art doesn't count,' they said. 'Why don't you give it up?'
(Better to be some wanker with a First
from Cambridge than a Michelangelo?)
I gave the lot up and went in for Art.
I'll wash my own brains, thank you very much.

[4]

Boys' Pockets

Storybooks tell us a boy's pocket's lined
with marbles, toffees, pen-knives and pet mice –
they never seem to mention condoms though.
And yet, I hear, most carry them around
like talismans until they drop to bits.

The vicar's son in Dylan Thomas's class
put in a mammoth order for them all
to be delivered to the vicarage,
my mother tells me. (She was Swansea bred.)

I've only felt in a boy's pocket once.
(When I was ten.) His arm was in a sling.
He said that he'd just broken it and asked
if I could get his handkerchief for him.
The pocket had the bottom torn right out.

Playing Games

In games the most you gain for your lost time's
a trifling win. I taught myself Chess young
to pretend I was intellectual,
but never play it now. I've mortgaged all
in Monopoly, lost tricks at cards,
lowered the tone of Scrabble.

As a child, I enjoyed games of logic –
I'd be Sherlock Holmes solving a strange case,
or a QC defending 'Lord Teddy'
on sex charges. (He always left threads
of his tartan trousers on the briers beside
the raped and murdered doll-victims.)

At school, I was indifferent at Games.
All I got from Lacrosse was a black eye.
I could not understand team spirit
or the urge to pat a ball across a net.
The 'sports' all fought dirty, kicked on target –
usually rectums or fannies – the rest
of us just strangled, wrestled and pulled hair
in a more aimless sort of way.

Later, I played at disillusioning
prim men, kidding myself they'd asked for it
by being humourless or shockable.
I even gave one straightlaced guy some tea
out of a teapot I made at sixteen –
it has four legs, a pot belly, bug eyes.
The sight of Earl Grey sputtering through
its broken teeth, half in the cup, half out,
sent him running home. I told Tories
that I was Communist, made Philistine
remarks to cultured types and wore tarty
get-ups for the religious ones. It seemed
more fun than simply saying no.

Others played Disillusionment and won –
my kink could hardly be unique. The ones
who turned homosexual or paedophile,
sadists, fascists who wished to shoot miners,
were all perhaps good straight men underneath.

I've dropped all games now, and I make my face
a mask that doesn't show the disbelief
I found so funny in my turn.

Beards

I have doubts about kissing men with beards.
It seems like cunnilingus when their lips
protrude from mousy hair.

Most women have brown pubics, even blondes.
I know this from my four years at Art School.
Once though, we had a model whose hair was all
the brightest shade of red against white skin.

The teacher, with his curly, mousy beard –
more like the real thing than hers – arranged
her propped on one hip in a cold-sheeted,
blue-white bed, tipped up like a fishmonger's
marble slab, chalking her pose on the cloth.

Through the weeks that followed, we saw her bruise
like a plum through the weight of her body.
And the brown-bearded teacher asked me why
I was more interested in structure than
the sensual texture of her skin.

A Strip of Fur

A Foundation student with long blue nails
suddenly took off into collage and,
pulling a Band Aid and fur from her bag,
stuck them (artistically) upon her nude.

Now, lecturers usually pretend
great tolerance, talk about 'What is Art?'
and stretch the definition to include
happenings, curtains across valleys and bricks.

This was too much though – a member of the
almost-all-male painting staff strode across
and scalped her picture's pubics; curiously
though, he left the Elastoplast intact,
leaving before comment was possible.

It was rumoured she went into Fashion.
Being naively-dedicated we
all thought that served her right.

Drag Act

Ralph West, my hall of residence, held
a beauty show for men in women's clothes,
enjoyed by all except one student who
complained that they were dressed, for he'd seen acts
in Paris wearing only sellotape.

The subtler types with mousy curls, eye-gloss
and tights took all the first places. The ones
with melons up their sweaters just got laughs.
A skirted slob with a black beard came last –
like some old pirate in a dead girl's clothes.

Later, that fatso, back in macho guise
ascended to a women's floor – the men
were odd, while we were even – knocked my door
and asked to borrow coffee. Naively, I went
to get the jar. He pushed me on the bed.
I hadn't noticed him before he donned
falsies and skirt. I didn't know his name.
Strangely, he looked more female in his clothes –
a flabby-breasted, breathless bearded lady,
trying, pathetically to prove himself a man,
feeling the need on that night to seem
threatening to someone, not just a laugh.

I threw him off and got him to the door.
As men will do, he tried to shift the blame,
saying, 'You looked as if you wanted it.'

Paris

Art History thought we ought to have a trip,
the second term in our Foundation Course –
Paris, a sort of long weekend, mainly
to do the Musée d'Art Moderne and Louvre.

The first night there, we tried to catch the mood
by playing strip poker in a small café
a local postman took us to. The game
went on and on and nothing was exposed.
I lost the most – a scarf and both my shoes.

I went around alone the next two days –
did all the Art as quickly as I could,
got off at almost every Metro stop,
picked up and dropped a lot of seedy men –
I was eighteen and it was Spring.
(Paris has little London hasn't got.
I could have done that lot back home –
just slightly different paintings, different men.)

Montmartre – back with my friends on the last night.
We met some artists of the bereted sort –
their work all looked several decades behind.
I talked in bloody awful schoolgirl French.

I had my photo taken on our way
to catch the coach next morning, doing things
to some statue. It didn't come out.

Nothing[3]

'A woman's nothing if she is not loved.
Nothing!' (I am not loved – therefore I'm not.
It follows, Q.E.D.)

This nothing sat and watched Coco Chanel
talking a load of crap on Channel Four.
She should have stuck to clothes.

I'm sick of women who boost those creatures Men –
make *them* directors, *us* auditioners
for the plum role of heroine-cum-drudge.

Love's just an inconvenience on the side
of life – more *nothing* than a woman is.
Women can live, give birth, grow old and die
without being loved – many of us will.

DIY

'They say vibrators are so good today
there's no more need for men . . .'
A nervous lecturer shot me his line.

How much does any woman *need* a man?
A test-tubeful of sperm could be a Dad.
We can all make the earth move on our own.
Men should do more to recommend themselves.

What do *they* want? I often ask myself.
Good looks? Good cooking? Sex and sympathy?
Market research among my friends reveals
that men are often most considerate
to women who can offer them free homes.

DIY's such a safe alternative to them –
no clap, no pox, no herpes, AIDS or crabs –
friggers can always come and don't have kids.

The foreplay though is rather short on fun –
how much of your own body can you kiss?

Meaningful Relationships

I've had no meaningful relationships –
the sort where both of you sit down and talk,
discussing when the time is ripe for sex,
then go to see a doctor, hand in hand,
so he or she can show you both the range
available to adult lovers now.
(*Hers* are the intra-uterine device –
plastic or metal – several different shapes,
the pessaries, the caps, the packs of pills.
His is the sheath – clinics of course don't stock
the coloured ones with frills – the National Health
wouldn't spend ratepayers' cash on kinks.)
Few of the men I've known have stopped to ask
what anti-life insurance I am on.

Martin

Nine gins and he was mine. He wasn't much good.

Two years before, I'd really fancied him –
drinks after work, sometimes the cinema –
but very little else . . .

That party night he came back to my flat;
I had him just to see what I had missed.

Men think about sex three times every hour,
psychologists have said. Some only think.
You have to get them drunk for any more.

Chivalry

When I was buying my tom-cat turkey legs
the butcher cut himself and muttered 'Damn!',
then, 'Sorry to swear in front of a lady.'

'Don't worry,' I said. 'I do it all the time.'
He stared. 'And does your husband do it too?'
'I haven't one.' 'Perhaps that's why!' he said.

Falling Down

I fell on the shallow sharp stone main stairs
of the British Museum. Two men who'd paused
looked shocked and hurried off when I yelled 'Fuck!'

I sat there shaken, nursing bruised fingers,
and wondered why my Anglo-Saxon shout
had lost me sympathy from that prim pair.
They must have done it in their time and yet
could not take a reminder of the root of life
in such a place and from a woman.

Soon, the entrance hall returned to normal –
conversations restarted – schoolchildren
and tourists trekked in search of mummies, cards,
the Elgin Marbles.

Raising The Dead

Seventeen years ago I saw a boy
pulled from the bottom of a swimming bath.
All of us there got out and watched a man
use mouth to mouth to bring him round.

The child spewed yellowed water on the edge
and screamed with fear at coming back to life.

This week I saw a tramp drop on the road.
He'd stood there waiting at the lights to cross
by Seven Dials. The lights went green. He fell
straight back and died. A tourist knelt to give
the kiss of life; her scarf trailed on the ground.

I crossed from the Long Acre side. Feeling
incredibly relieved she'd got there first,
(I'm no St Francis-type), I went to buy
my Christmas cards.

Fortunes

A friend had a nine quid crystal ball job
on Hastings Pier. Months later she was glad,
she said, the job changes had not come through.
It meant she wouldn't have to have three kids.

My twenty-five pence one – told to me
in the Labour Party's annual jumble sale
by a ringleted old ex-dancer
with a hernia, who prescribed Epsom Salts
to keep the figure, cold tea for the hair –
did not come true. It was *too* good – I thought
that at the time – all cash and men, rewards
for sympathetic listening to her tale
of how she'd once lived next to Mrs T.
and heard *all* about her from her daily.

Truth's too bizarre for palms and crystal balls;
my hands are pale and lacking half the lines;
and fortune-teller's guesses are too safe
for lives like mine.

Another year I went back to that sale
wanting five-bob's-worth more of laughs.
Only the jumble stalls remained, badges,
posters. The fortune teller'd gone.

Uncle Andrew

My Uncle Andrew said he wouldn't look
at women over forty years of age.
He'd picked a quarrel with my Mum by then,
when I was one. (I saw him last at eight.)
He'd never 'been caught'. He used to give rich wives
of richer men than he rich gifts and played
godfather to their sons at public schools.
He died alone.

We kept a token correspondence up –
just birthdays, thank-you letters, Christmas cards.
He boasted once how he'd outlived my Dad
and sent a box of Edinburgh Rock.

His later letters looked like telegrams –
one-page, one-lines, all in capitals –
MY LITTLE DOG IS DEAD AND I FEEL OLD.

At 79, he sent a photo of himself –
young, handsome, smiling and in uniform.
The doctor rang to check up on his past.
They said he was 'confused'. He changed his name
back to the one he'd hated all his life.
(I joked of 'Nuncle Horace' to my Mum.)
We visualised him flashing in his kilt –
Perth's kirkyard's bogle, leaping down from tombs.
They kept him in three weeks, then sent him home.
His last note asked about my father's death.

In March, the last three women in his life
all telephoned. The nurse said he was dead.
The doctor thought it might have been TB
and asked if a post mortem was OK.
Then, finally, his social-worker rang.
A very bourgeois Scot, she talked
of paupers' funerals and unmarked graves.

Just Good Friends

I'm the 'just friendship' one –
the other Other Woman in his life.
I get to hear about the *other* two.

He says his wife's too old at 45
for sex. He has a girl of 24 for that.
He calls her 'brainless' – she forgets the Pill.
He jokes about leading her on to try
odd kinks that make her look ridiculous.

I'm told he's never mixed friendship and sex.
His wife like me's a friend. They haven't had
much sex and none of it was any good.
She doesn't clean the place or cook for him,
or put a penny into paying bills.
'I run a one-man charity,' he says.
She doesn't care a fuck about his work.
She's scratched his face, given him various knocks,
torn a review-copy to little bits,
plays rather funny little jokes on him –
like lying round pretending to be dead.
Last time he told me problems on the phone
I heard her yelping like a terrier.
'She's frigid,' he says.

The roofing bloke he paid to stay with her
and do the roof while he was off with Mum
was just 'a friend'. The roof still leaks.
The man with a tattoo across his face
who turned up in their bedroom once, was just
'a friend'. She goes to several private views a night,
tells him she's off to use a word-processor
(belonging to a friend) at 1 a.m.

He thinks that I should give up 'using men',
in fact, give them *all* up, just be his friend.
He talked of *Brief Encounter* in the pub.
I'm his 'white kitten' too. We're just good friends.
I'm welcome in his house to stay the night.
(I'll take a rain-check on that though – for fear
of meeting tattooed men.)

What do I hang on for? The 'Love' he puts
upon the letters that he sometimes writes?
The 'Love and admiration' on his books?
The sighing pauses on the telephone?
His hand upon my cheek, his lips on mine?
Blue eyes? He's quite a handsome shit.

Mills and Boon

The Midlands Arts Centre in Birmingham
hosted a lecture for the Festival,
on Mills and Boon.

An editress and author gave a talk –
like two American evangelists.
We Moonies sat there drinking it all in.
Too many Regency, too few Renaissance men –
they're slightly short of costume romance plots.
These days the heroines are allowed careers;
Doctor and Nurse can now be Doc plus Doc.
We were advised to study lots of books
before we sent in our first manuscript.
(Aha, I thought, you've got the innocents –
housewives who want a gentle mental-wank,
so now you're going round the festivals
to rope in more pretentious literary shites.)
They'd have us *all* reading and writing the stuff.

Their table had three piles beside the jugs.
One handout told us how to type our book –
some useful tips – like numbering from 1.
Another said what contents were allowed.
The third was just a little order form
for the cassette.

Then came the question-time – a welcome break.
A fattish person in the top back left
wanted to know why they'd rejected hers
when she had followed every single rule
and women's magazines just loved her stuff.

Others showed much willingness to set to work,
queried the pay. (They didn't get to know.)
The local author though dropped subtle hints –
she had a word-processor and microwave
and now was 'one-up in the housing-chain'.
Some asked what sort of girl . . . what sort of man . . .
All sounded Saved as Billy Graham's flock.
I meant to be a Devil's advocate
and said I didn't like their brutal males.
The author told me she'd had 'thirty-seven
affairs' with them – the people in her books.
An addict zombie murmured fervently,
'My neighbour lent me a whole pile of them –
I was in plaster to the hip – I thought
the heroes were all *lovely* men.'
I was outnumbered evidently.
The editress intent on winning my soul –
she saw me as an author for her lot –
took it I didn't like this modern sex,
and told me a nice old scenario
about a widower with two small kids
who slept rooms from his bride on The First Night.
I had to say 'Perhaps he was impotent
and doped her cocoa just to cover up.'
She didn't like my theory all that much.

We should be careful what we fantasise –
it might, it *really* might come true at last.
I've tried to see myself within those books.
'Mills and Boon heroines don't sleep around!'
we'd heard. 'They're 17 to 28.'
None of that audience even qualified.

I'm more the hero type, I'd have to say –
tall, dark and handsome, powerful (if not rich).
I should get some young, trembling, virgin bloke,
crush him against a wall in a hotel
(in some exotic spot) and bruise his lips.
Then, chapters on, after an argument,
I'd dominate him in the lift, get one
strong hand inside his silken shirt and tear
the buttons off – no hassle, he can sew.
I'd feel his nipples harden at my touch.
The other hand would grasp his slender nape.
I'd press against him with my powerful frame.
His mouth would open slowly under mine.
(He'd feel exquisite torture all the while.)
In the last chapter when things are resolved,
I'd scoop him up and chuck him on the bed.
(My art school days and frequent DIY
have made me quite exceptionally strong.)
He'd smell the perfume of a thousand flowers –
he'd know I'm single, know that I'm his boss.
As I bore down, I'd hear his 'Show me how . . .'
But no, I've got it wrong it's 'We must wait!'
'Show me how' 's only for The Wedding Night.
The virgin bloke's a mercenary bitch.

The Mask

After my grandpa's death, my father found
a Chinese cardboard mask and copy
of Krafft-Ebbing locked in Newnes's office safe.

Respectably alcoholic, 'Old Vic'
read his 'review copies' though *The Wide World*
never did reviews, drank champagne solo
and indulged in japes of an Edwardian
character – painting extra figures
in a convincing style on Christmas cards
to freak the guests. Not content with editing,
he'd talk of writing other books. (His first,
written under other names – The Captain,
Sidney York, Rupert Chesterton
and Singleton Carew – were ripping yarns
where villains smuggled saccharin, or tales
of lands where the heroes always cried
'Caramba!', Incas or derring-do at sea.)

Twice weekly he would take the train to work,
passing his friend, a retired editor,
rearing rhubarb at Rickmansworth with young
and pretty 'Nursie' at his side (his heart
was bad). As the train slowed Vic would rise, wave
in some new disguise, his George-Burns-face screwed
up as Nelson, a penny at one eye,
arm in a sling and a paper cocked hat.
Then he'd put the lot away and sit back.
Tailored and toupéed – he was the perfect
image of the City gent, till sickness
took him on that journey where there are
no masks – no Fu Manchu or Charlie Chan
to hide behind.

Love Hate Relationships

Love-hate relationships just don't exist.
Sadists invented the idea so they
could have a nail to hang their cruelty on,
put in the boot then patch it up with sex,
simulate tenderness like succubi.

Some separate the objects of their hate
from all their real allies, trap them alone
like victims of Victorian poisoners,
fuck up their friendships, treat their guests like shit.

Their poor conned partners say it's justified,
put up with all as all gets worse and worse –
the jibes, the ripped-up books, the violence,
so they can try to kid the world they're loved.
(They've even half-convinced themselves.)

Phone Call

'I am a poet, and . . .' my caller paused
(in doubt perhaps?) 'I *think* that you're one too.
Poets should meet. I'm quite respectable –
I have a wife and daughter of fifteen
and run a Brighton language school.'

(What did he think was in a date for me?
I'll show you mine if you will show me yours?)

I'd had my photo in the *Sunday Telegraph*
that day, together with an interview.
He slipped out while his wife was cooking lunch.
The call-box pips cut through.

He'd got his family and well-paid job
and thought he'd rather like to have my fame.

I've met his type. I know those seaside schools –
a seedy Summer world of Jack-the-lads
who try to pull the under-age.

I talked of years of being under-paid,
of writing forty hours in every week,
subsisting on the dole or part-time jobs,
notching up hundreds of rejection slips
to gain the small acceptance I have now.
Poetry's not just something on the side.

Gents Only [4]

Amongst my quota of rejection slips,
(Some kind some not, some with subscription pleas
Or bumf on festivals and literary trips),
Two stand alone – an ancient MBE's.
After placatory statements not to offend
A potential reader, both letters end
Describing meeting me outside the Gents.
The Gents indeed! Unlikeliest of events.
I do not haunt such evil piss-stale dens,
Where flashers lurk and male tarts ply their trade,
And pederasts pursue the under-tens,
Offering them chocolate cake or lemonade.

Still, in a funny way, he had it right.
The literary world is full of piss and shite
By men. For years I lurked outside that door,
Waiting my chance to go and do some more,
Legs crossed and desperate to let it flow,
Without a bloody penny for the slot,
While inside, all the bastards in a row,
Stood envying what the man next door had got.

Big Pricks

Last birthday someone sent a glossy card –
a headless torso graced the frontside fold,
solarium-tanned an even reddish-brown.
Inside the centre bit, its droopy dong
hung like a leathered rope on hairy thighs.

A naked man can turn me on I find –
a well-developed chest, a tightish bum,
long legs . . . a general harmony of form.
I'm choosy though – he has to have a head.
Big pricks are over-rated bits of meat.

Priapic worship's more a game for men –
they're big – they think they've won the pools at birth.

I knew a theatre usher long ago
who liked to boast that he could suck his own.
Large cocks are good for narcissism, not sex.
Their owners have this tendency to stand
as if they're waiting for a prize at Cruft's.
'What a big boy! Aren't I the lucky girl?'
we're meant to say. They're Ozymandias-like
about their things.

Double Standards[3]

Though all agree that frequent exercise
will make the stomach, thighs and bottom taut,
fannies, they'd ask us to believe, given
the same regime go slack.

'Licked bread and butter' is a phrase that some
men like to use. They should remember that
the lower half of an ageing sandwich tastes
less dried-up and disgusting than the top.
They're like bent knockers trying to get us cheap.
Aladdin's lamp's despised as secondhand.
The patina of pearls worn next to skin
is wasted on their eyes.

Hands that have used a wide variety
of tools are labelled 'skilled'. Experience counts
in *everything*.

Posing

Once David Bailey stated on TV
people with bodies that were beautiful
had no objection to appearing nude.
(We never see *him* on a calendar.)

Sarah, an art school model, showed
her bum in Chelsea's King's Road's Odeon –
a protest that the Ladies loo in there
was permanently out of bumf. (She got
Drunk and Disorderly topped with *Contempt* –
for telling the tale in Court.)

Page 3 girls only seem to show their tits.
They always keep at least a G-string on.
Miss World is even more respectable.
She wears a swimsuit and when questioned says
she'd like to help the Handicapped and Old.

Our bodies have to be a certain type.
Sagged flesh is always thought much more obscene.
The topless girls in the Old Vic's *Bacchae*
had sloppy breasts. 'You'd think they'd hold them back
with sellotape!' the ushers' cashier said.

An extra hired for *Steaming*'s sauna scenes,
(15 quid bonus on her chit for showing all),
when told to drop her towelling wrap refused
implicitly. She had a lot to hide –
her knickers, bra, vest, jumpers, skirt and coat.

'1984'

We Party Members stood and cheered Big Brother
on Victory Square in '1984'.
A smiling soldier, imaged on two screens,
worked his way down a line of hostages,
blowing their heads off like ripe melons.
We applauded him and raised our arms
in a diaphragm-wrenching crossed-fist salute.

A gangway was cleared through the crowd. Lorries
edged forward on their caterpillar tracks
across the mud. Inside were prisoners.
The Asian extras stood, feet bare
on the cold metal of the Army vans,
their legs in irons. We'd seen them painted by girls
squeezing their blood make-up from small foil tubes.
We'd queued with them for soup. And we cried out
'Kill! Kill! Death! Death!' through many takes. We stood
close in the pre-dawn chill and met their eyes
each time the trucks stopped by the mass gallows.

At first light it was all over. Faces
relaxed. The boiler-suits and heavy boots
were handed back to the Wardrobe.
Victims and oppressors, one in acted hate,
were paid the same.

Bond Girl

Back in my extra days, someone once swore
she'd seen me in the latest James Bond film.

I tried to tell her that they only hired
the really glamorous leggy types for that.
(My usual casting was 'a passer-by'.)

I've passed the lot in Pinewood Studios.
It's factory-like, grey aluminium, vast
and always closed. Presumably that's where
they smash up all the speedboats, cars and bikes
we jealous viewers never could afford.)

I quite enjoyed the books. Ian Fleming wrote well.
I could identify *a touch* with Bond,
liking to have adventure in my life.
The girls were something else. All that they earned
for being perfect samples of their kind –
Black, Asian, White – blonde, redhead or brunette,
groomed, beauty-parlourised, pleasing in bed,
mixing Martinis that were shaken not stirred,
using pearl varnish on their nails not red –
was death. A night (or 2) with 007,
then they were gilded till they could not breathe,
chucked to the sharks, shot, tortured, carried off
or found, floating face downward in a pool.

Prostitution[5]

My *Sky Ray Lolly* was a hit, they said –
few thousand sales, six hundred quid for me.
My *Private Parts* will do as well, it seems.

Chatto's my pimp. My cut is five per cent
(well in arrears). Clause after clause decrees
I earn less still and part's kept back for years.

I'm published now, so spin-offs come my way –
performances – I'm paid from fifty to
a hundred pounds for every one-night stand.
Some buggers think that I should do it free.

I also tout my work around the place.
My clientele is small but most select –
George wanted twenty for the BBC,
Karl's had a lot of it at thirty quid,
Hugo and Blake have settled for a few.

It all adds up . . .

It's time to tell the world about my 'job'.
Last year I made about two thousand net.
This year if I am lucky, I'll make three –
too much for dole, less than a cleaner's wage.

I've taken off my clothes for many men,
but never felt as naked then as now.

I'm 33 and can't afford to rent
the smallest bedsit on my salary.
I live with Mum. Our house is stinking damp
and almost everything we own is old –
no, not antique – just *fucking* secondhand.

What should I do, what chances do I have?
Arvon – the poets' pools? (Yes, we all try.)
The odds are twenty thousand though, to one.

The under-thirties Gregory Awards?
(Twenty to women out of 144.)
I was turned down for one of those six times.
Anthony Thwaite seems guilty on that score –
since Chatto took me up at least – he rang
my editor to say it wasn't *his* fault.

The Cholmondley and the Hawthornden? They're both
awards where no submissions can be made.
Some men sit round a table, I am told.
Perhaps I'm wrong, perhaps I'm being unjust –
I wonder if they give them to their friends.

Of course, the Arts Council does grants . . . just three.
But '87 was Caribbean Year,
so every applicant *had to be* black.

One option I have left's to turn to prose.
(Nobody books me to adjudicate:
nobody wants me to anthologise.)

Fiction, I hear, can raise some decent cash –
a brief synopsis brings a good advance.
Half a collection wouldn't raise a p.

Novels have twice the pages, far more words
so editors can write between the lines
to justify *their* jobs.

I do a lot to earn my five per cent.
My brothel's tucked away in Bedford Square.
Bad pay does not breed loyalty.

I deal with piles of letters from my fans –
most need replies. A stamp and envelope
wipe out the price I'm paid for one book's sale.

I get more letters from my editors,
sudden requests of the peremptory kind –
query on query, meetings, calls on calls –
300 words on why I did the book,
a new CV, a photo or a form.
And everything is needed by return.

'Gifted and strikingly original'
my whorehouse/sweatshop dubbed me in one blurb.
'Gifted and strikingly original'
does not bring in a greater flow of cash.
Even their typists get a better screw.

South African Interview

The South African *Cosmopolitan*
wanted an interview. 'Would I? Could I?'
Chatto and Windus asked. I thought I could.
Books aren't like fruit, I reasoned to myself,
not buying or selling keeps information back.

I met the journalist. Her grandfather'd
built a cathedral over there, she said.
She'd lived in Bristol though, for years.

We had a meal, then the photographer
turned up. He wanted me to stand beside
a neon mouth on one of Soho's clubs,
and then, some classier shots outside a church.
He used a lens 'to warm the colours up.'

A friendly down-and-out whose bench we'd pinched
took me aside and pointed to a grave –
'The only one the Council haven't moved.
He used to be the King of Corsica.
I don't know why he ended up down here.'
He turned to the photographer.

'Nice camera. Are you Americans?
Well, Aussies then?' 'We're from South Africa.'

'South Africa! So what's it like out there?'
I thought he'd say the weather and the food
were good. His face became quite closed.
'It's all over.' He started walking off.
'It's over now. It's *all* over now!'

'Who won? What's-is-name Botha, I suppose.'

AIDS

Condoms can never save the world from germs –
machines run out of them and chemists close;
a friend blames two abortions on the things;
some funny little foreign ones don't fit;
besides, they're not much use for oral sex.

Evangelists rejoice God's got the gays.
(He's let off lesbians though – and wankers too –
of course, we all know *they* go blind.)

A dinner-party back I heard it all.
'It came from Haiti where men go with pigs.'
'The CIA invented it in labs
to kill the Reds. There was an accident . . .'
'The Government should shoot the lot of them.'
'It's haemophiliacs that I'm sorry for . . .'
Then some Scots poet did his little piece –
four lines about an AIDS-infected fart.
He'd written it on the way down from Arbroath –
specially for the Hastings Festival,
with one (in grunts) about a spastic boy.

We're all immune (or not) to certain things.
Half of the class gets measles, half does not.
We're all sentenced to death. There's no reprieve.
Whom the gods love die early? Some from AIDS.

Whitelaw's Commission says we 'must be made
to think monogamy's the correct way.'
Mr and Mrs Right have married bliss
(and one point seven kids). The rest of us
must chop and change.

Safe sex? There's no such thing.

[40]

Defending Rats

'I don't know what I'm doing defending rats!'
a barrister once said to me. He'd tired
of rapist clients who blamed it on TV.
Why weren't they influenced by *Songs of Praise?*
His last, a case of oral sex by force, had left
'a nasty taste'.

Most rats, of course, don't end up in a Court,
don't need a paid professional defence.
I've made excuses for the men I've liked –
their oafishness was tiredness or 'flu;
their crass remarks were pressure at work or home;
their cancellations, mild insanity.

Last week the latest rodent in my life
wiped two whole years of friendship out
with 'I despise you thoroughly' . . .
'I never want to hear your stupid voice again.'

I try to think
some programme must have driven him to the act.
(His favourite show's *The Sullivans* I know.)
Rats can't be held responsible.

Family Affairs

Sex in a porno book is always good –
the cocks all stand, the cunts are full of cream.

Hot Sucking Sitter is my friend's best friend.
(A paperback she bought in Amsterdam –
she uses it to turn her toy boy on.
She lent me the damned thing to read, saying
she'd need it back. The corner was all chewed.)
Son buggers Mom while she's on top of Dad;
Dad sucks the sitter cos she'd felt left out.
(Son was the teenage baby that she'd sat.)

My father's favourite had a gentler theme.
Herbert was kept at home too long by Mum;
she made him wear long combs till middle age;
he went to college then and picked up girls.
He had a different one for every day,
Val – Monday, Tuesday – Anne, et cetera.
They left their dresses hanging in his room
and they were all size 10 – that's 32
around the chest, which seemed a little odd
because elsewhere we read they had big breasts.

Men often see lovers or wives as Mums
who've kept them babied up away from all
the more exciting times they could have had
with partners fit to fill their fantasies –
Page Threes.

I can admire beauty in female forms
as well as male – good models I have drawn,
The Rokeby Venus, statues in museums
and various actresses in various films.
Page Threes, these days, are more an anagram –
like schoolgirls sporting nursing-mothers' tits.

Who likes that mixture? Well, it's obvious – a lot
of unweaned, would-be daughter-fucking Dads.

Ken Roberts

Ken Roberts rings me up to ask if I
like going to the cinema alone –
and, like a fool, I stop and talk to him.

He says he bets that he could turn me on.
(I bet he can't.) I say this, but it's hard
to put his kind of bubbly pervert down.

Do I enjoy it when a stranger puts
his hand upon my knee during the film?
'No, only old and ugly men do that!'
I say. He tells me that he's 46.

He says he *sees* me at the kitchen sink
in stockings and a short bright blue silk dress
and slides his hand from stocking-top to thigh.
What would I do? he asks.

'I'd tip my dirty water over you.'
'I *think* I'd like you doing that,' he says.
'Oh no you wouldn't,' I say, 'it's full of grease
and nasty sticky little bits of food.'
'Oh yes I would!' Ken says.

Playing House

In Swansea, in her youth, my mother used
to play in a large field full of small stones.
The children gathered these and set them out
like the foundations of a two-roomed house
with gaps for doors.

They sat on large flat stones
inside and ate their sandwiches or sweets.
The girls cradled their dolls to bed on grass
until the rougher boys charged through the midst
and kicked the walls away.

Some couples stick like kids at Playing House.
He's in the front, she's in the back. Each one's
intent on his, or her own game. They row
for 20, 30, 40, 50 years
without a Mum or Dad to smack their bums,
or dry their tears, and take them home.

Swan Song

Men like to tell me stories of the lives
and loves of birds. I don't know why. The last –
a lonely widower – told me about
a pair of swans he'd fed and almost tamed.
They used to come for dried-up hunks of bread.
The hen was shot, leaving the cob alone.
(He was an oldish bird with a scarred beak.)

One day, two other swans came sailing by.
She was a beauty, young enough to have
grey down still left upon her head. 'A trace –
a bit like eyeshadow,' he said.

The ancient bird beat up the younger cob
and stole his mate.

I learnt this over business dinner for two.
Old Fat-and-Fifty'd tricked me out with him
by saying he had a client interested
in photographing his antiques against
the background of my house (restored for free).

Lies ask for lies.
I made a jealous boyfriend for myself,
one who'd resent my having dinner again.
The truth is I'm too nice, (or cowardly?),
to say I'm bored with going out with bores
and hate being seen with unattractive men.
(No boyfriend's ever cared a tuppenny fuck.)

Last week he rang again, offering advice –
insurance, pensions for the self-employed.
'I'm single and dependentless,' I said,
'so what's the point in doing anything?
I've nothing to invest. Besides, writers
just go on writing till they drop.'

Pen Friends[6]

Pen friends should be kept at a great distance.

Anthony does translations for the EEC.
He longed for me to share his three-wheeler car
to Barcelona for a conference.
It needed ballast for the mountain roads,
he said, endearingly.

Ian lives in the YMCA. He boasts
he has no friends and sends me 'articles' –
a hundred words or so in ballpoint pen –
on mini-skirts and how they cause VD.

Greville knows more about VD. He wrote
to tell me how he caught his NSU
(an East End pro – 'Teresa was her name').
And he enclosed his latest, *Listen With Mother*,
a story for the BBC about
a tape worm and an enema in love.

Three Johns came next. One left a souvenir
addressed to me – I'd read at Birmingham –
a xerox of *phallus impudicans*
commonly known as the stinkhorn mushroom.
I thought he'd photocopied something else
until I read the poem underneath.

Another John, ex-army oil-rigger,
who owned a purple car called Nazgûl once,
wrote of his new idea – a Sci Fi book
about a brothel for aliens on his rig.

And yet another John sent a prophetic piece
in rhyme, together with his photograph.
He was reclining in his caravan.
And (with my usual luck) he had a belly
beneath his tee shirt and combat jacket,
a pinkish towel wrapped about his waist,
a long black beard and lots of chains. And worse . . .
he threatened to visit me.

Lovebirds

I stood looking out on blossoming trees
through a tall window between stripped shutters.
He sat at the desk where he works each day
and talked of the blackbirds in his garden
and how they'd paired for life.

They sing quite sweetly, but it's hard to tell
the little clones apart. Perhaps we see
the things we want to see in animals.

The male went for small dull brown birds I thought,
while she, she probably has a long string
of black lovers, perhaps even invites back
the odd magpie or cuckoo to their nest.

Bodybuilding

While pumping iron at Hastings Sports Centre
a schoolboy used to chat to me. These days
I see the disillusion in his eyes
now I can pull more weight.

The back wall, right behind the sit-up board,
has dirty finger-marks across the white,
four screw-holes where the full-length mirror was
and posters of bronzed, over-muscled guys,
posed, bulging in the California sun.
He looks at these and asks the older men
how long it takes to get like that.

'Forty hours every week, at least, for life,'
one says. (That sounds like Poetry, I think.)
'It's narcissistic. They're not normal blokes.
They have to make a living out of comps.
You need a funny mind, plus the right frame.
I wish I'd started young – like you.'

Mr Hastings

We smelt the baby oil from the back row.
The 'Senior Mr Hastings' was judged first.
The oldest held a world above his head
(invisible) to music of the spheres.
The younger 'Mr Hastings' came on next,
'Miss Hastings' and 'Mr 1066'.

Every contestant does a short routine;
each has a tape – film theme tunes, classics, pop.
'This is the force of evil' pounds away –
we're told he's from a boys' club in the South.
One simpers like an odalisque and moves
seductively. The audience like his act.
(I'd seen him training once – a weekday night –
much butcher then, in baggy khaki shorts,
he sat and farted on the blue foam mat.)

A compère links it all with healthy talk.
'Mike trains in Pinks and Dave's from Genie's Gym . . .'
We're told we should encourage the young lads.
(The youngest and the weediest one had
'I vow to thee my country' on his tape.)

Some men and 'lads' went in for showmanship.
Nick finished his stint by roaring like a lion.
Goldfinger had a gilded condom on his hand
(until the thing slipped off).

The women, in a small class of their own,
did not wear trunks – G-string and bra combined.
(The halter laced from front to back to front.)
The man behind me shouted 'Show it, Debs!'
Debs won. She had a nice gold lamé job
with pleats like gilded scallop shells.

The interval was competition time –
the prize, a full year's adult membership
of Hastings Sports Centre. (That's worth £8.)
Competitors lifted a bucket up
containing a car battery and kept
it up as many seconds as they could . . .
We really heard them strain.

After the judging's done, Vince Brown comes on –
the guest star of the show. He's really huge.
The lights go down. He shows us how it's done
to disco beat and shouts of 'Beef it, Vince.'

I'd Like To Get You Back

You said that I'm 'not woman enough to hold a man' . . .

I'd dressed so carefully to please that day
in January – a tailored pencil skirt
(half of a suit you'd once admired),
a cashmere sweater, pale blue, soft to touch,
embroidered round the neck with rays of beads
in silvered glass and sequins overlapped
and clustered into flowers.

Your skin felt harsher when we kissed;
next moment you were looking at your watch.
I tried to keep things light, hang on with jokes.
Your tone, each sentence, showed you'd tired of me
and couldn't wait to finish brutally.
I sat and cried. You muttered 'For Christ's sake . . .'

Give me another chance, my love.
I've changed. I'm stronger. I can promise you
things will be very different this time round.

Now, I shall drink in praise, not be content,
angle for more. I'll make you jealous too,
play other men against you, one by one,
hint at the better times I've had with them.
I'll lead you on with looks, with words, with touch.

And when I'm sick of lapping kindness up,
I'll be the one to start to cancel dates,
claiming you paused while chatting on the phone,
so that I felt I *had to* ask you out.
(Do you remember what you said?)

At our last meeting in a crowded bar –
wear your best suit, try hard for me – I swear
I'll leave you crying for the love you lost.

Wet Dreams

'Bring me the sweat of Gabriela Sabatini' Clive James.

Clive James has written that he'd like to sup
Ms Sabatini's sweat served in a cup.
Betjeman first admired the type-athletic
Establishing a new female aesthetic.

Other poets have used odd themes like gadflies, lice,
Smallpox, the groin, the gut, arseholes or mice.
Yet, usually, they swallow better booze
Than drippings from armpits or tennis shoes.

I like to weight-train three times every week
And swim each day, unless the sea's too bleak.
Doing Sport's normal, watching it's perverse –
Just as with sex. A telly-wanker's worse.
I quote the case of Mr Lee who wears
His girlfriend's bra and pants for his affairs
With TV stars. While she goes out to shop
He turns Anne Diamond on and comes on top,
Then asks me if he's normal on the phone . . .
(Sometimes his voice subsides into a groan.)

Clive's not like that I'm sure. He wouldn't make tapes
Of Wimbledon for DIY home rapes.
(Blue movies of mixed doubles on the court?
Love Forty's far too many I'd have thought.)
He's on the box himself – a target too
For fetishists and sweatophiles to do.
A friend of mine has got the hots for him –
She's very kinky, red-haired, blue-eyed, slim
With *Star Bird* tits. I could give her address . . .
She's nine months pregnant though, I must confess.

[56]

I don't want anyone who's on TV.
The glass between's a barrier to me.
My wanking fantasies are fixed on men
I mean to have, have had, will have again.

Just for this poem's sake I'll play a game
We women play with friends. (It has no name.)
You look around the talent in a bar,
The old, the impotent, the under par,
Decide their merits slowly, one by one,
And which you'd have if threatened with a gun.
The men all sense that they are being admired,
Blush, bridle, look poetically inspired,
Unless they overhear us trying to choose
Between stained flies, toupées and pointed shoes.

Borg, Becker and the Brat – all B for bore.
(My temper's McEnroe enough for four.)
Sportsmen in sweatbands, shorts, shirts, socks and shoes
Have too much on. The Ancients didn't choose
Such overdressing down in the arena –
Nude exercise is funnier not obscener.

Imran Khan looks so good it seems a shame
I simply cannot bear to watch his game.
(The way those bowlers polish up the ball
Across their genitals – they're wankers all.)
Thompson in Rome still seemed to be at peak –
I would have given him gold – for his physique.

Enough of Sport. I'll turn my mind to Chat,
For politicians mostly are too fat.
Bragg? Harty? Wogan? Frost? No! No! No! No!
Dame Edna? Witty – he's got glasses though.
And Kilroy-Silk . . . Some say that he's a dish.
He's handsome, yes, but smugger than I'd wish.

The Theatre and Film are full of looks –
As myriad as the swearwords in my books.
It's hard to know which stars I should select:
Young British Lions? Hollywood's Elect?
I quite like Superman though he wears tights,
Irons and Everett could warm my nights.
Brando was beautiful till too much grub
Altered his manly shape. Now, there's the rub –
A fan can *only* see the idol fall,
Go off, deteriorate and start to pall.

Clive James, I feel that I must call your bluff.
Pull Gabriela – you are good enough.
Women are kind. She might indulge your kink.
(I've gratified some funnier ones, I think.)
A weekend's sauna should yield up a gill –
Several weekends and you could have your fill.
Worship is not a patch on real-life sex,
So throw away your rosy-tinted specs.
Constructing odes will never serve your turn;
She's not some painting on a Grecian urn.
Remember all the tales great Ovid wrote –
Goddesses love to fuck – don't miss the boat!

The National Health

'When the National Health first started,' he said,
'her brother went and got the lot from them:
glasses for seeing, glasses for reading,
a double set of teeth, a wig, a sponge . . .
And then, he died.'

Notes on the Poems

When I was a child I thought that being an author meant that you sat down and wrote books and people published them. In 1978, I went over to writing full-time. A few years of failure taught me that you could write books and not have them published. In 1986 when my first collection – apart from some small press efforts – was published, I became an author in most people's eyes. I very soon found out writing is not like any other job.

Before *Sky Ray Lolly* was published I had only received two or three fan letters and absolutely no dirty phone calls. Things have certainly changed. A writer's lot is not an easy one. Editors had spoken to me of strong reactions to my work. Karl Miller of the *London Review of Books* was once threatened that 'God would strike him down' if he continued to publish me. Blake Morrison told of many wives writing in to the *Observer* to claim for their own the husbands I had satirised in a poem called *Married Men*. Unfortunately, these letters are not extant. The only amusing letter about my poems that I have been able to lay my hands on was written by an MP.

Fan letters sent directly to myself are not always as funny. Their range is enormous though. Their writers vary in age from fourteen to eighty-nine. They include vicars, a vicar's daughter, an oil-rigger, a kitchen fitter, teachers, civil servants, gardeners, astrologers, bankers, doctors, paedophiles, artists, musicians, fellow-writers, lunatics and wankers. Some fans are unemployed and so have time to write twenty pages in cramped biro. Long missives are a nuisance, because they can take half an hour to decipher. Sometimes the letters come smelling of roses, Devon violets or, in one case, TCP. At the moment my post averages one fan letter a day.

If a newspaper runs a profile on me this usually produces a crop of letters and callers. It's interesting to see the character differences between readers of various papers. The *Independent* brought a large batch of letters but no phone calls. A bad review in the *Spectator* brought letters of sympathy from a lord and a major. *Today* brought me Mr Lee (he's mentioned in *Wet Dreams*), plus someone who told me he was so gorgeous I would want to sleep with him as soon as I saw what he had. I told him he didn't sound gorgeous and put the phone down. I can't resist answering back. Mr Lee, on the other hand, belonged to the category of men who was seeking my advice as a kind of unofficial agony aunt. It's hard to refuse this, because some of these characters seem almost suicidally depressed. Usually I regret putting up with such men when the letters or the phone calls continue. Mr Lee rang a total of eight times. Another depressed man wrote to me recently, complaining that he was twenty-four and had never been kissed because he was so ashamed of his body. I wrote him a long sympathetic letter advising him to take up weight-training and make his body look the way he wanted it to be. I got the reply that the trouble wasn't with his pectorals, but his testicles.

Colour supplements usually bring out the beast in my fans. They are a prime trigger for heavy breathers and men demanding dates. I don't want to go out on blind dates, but I have had a hard job explaining this at times. Two men tricked me out with them on the basis of business propositions after a *Sunday Times* profile. One of these is mentioned in *Swan Song*. The other was a Greek film producer who waltzed off with one of my manuscripts and has never returned it.

Strangest of all, my mother was once sent a somewhat unintelligible letter. It appeared to be a collection of pieces in favour of child-abuse. The sentences were so long and surreal-istic though, it was hard to tell. On the outside of the envelope, the anonymous sender had written: 'Thank you for Fiona's soft centre.'

*

This was the letter from the MP, retrieved by a friend of a mole in the library service:

5th December, 1987

Dear Mr Collis,
I have been approached by constituents who tell me that a pornographic poetry book is available in the Central Milton Keynes Children's Library. I was horrified to hear this and to hear extracts from it. The book in question is *Skyraid Lolly* [sic] and, from the cover, would appear to be a children's book, but the contents are certainly not for children. It struck me that possibly the books are not being vetted sufficiently and I would be most grateful to have your comments.

Yours sincerely,

W. BENYON. M.P.

In an article in the *Sunday Times* (December 1987) where various people were asked about Christmas presents, I mentioned briefly that I had once written a note to Santa in green crayon asking for a good fuck. The *Sunday Times* being a nice family paper I was forced to put 'a synonym for fornication' instead of good old-fashioned Anglo-Saxon. Six months later I received the following letter from a vicar:

Dear Ms Pitt-Kethley
You are an artist in words, a poet, and as such please look up 'fornication' in the Dictionary. When you wrote to Santa in green crayon you might have thought that it meant 'fuck' (the noun) as the Americans have been thinking for some 50 years – but you are grown up now. How could what Donne calls 'the right true end of love' be a deadly sin? or a sin at all of any degree? You know that this gift of God is a good thing.

[62]

After the publication of my second collection, *Private Parts*, I received the following:

Dear Miss Pitt-Kethley,
A very good afternoon. May I say that I completely agree with you regarding your thoughts on men. I can confirm that most well, 95% I should think are complete bastards, excuse the language.
Their greatest allegiance and devotion (that is their only) is with their mates weird though that may be.
It's the way life has evolved on this planet that men as a male or breed are obnoxious whilst women are quite the opposite, I'm only looking at the facts, just the facts, I suppose I retain a certain objectivity by being a male but there it is.
If you feel you're completely isolated in merely pointing out inwards what most men are and especially in the great gulf between them and women characterwise, that's no big deal since it's the strength of an argument rather than how isolated it is in its voice even if that's against the whole world, that counts. That's the voice of a 4 year old and 25 year old now in 1987. Yes one finds oneself walking around saying what? Cold, clinical, and above logical reasoning says, it's in the genes of animals and humans, a little genetic engineering and you could find yourself quite a guy even if by biological standards, this specimen would be a terrible mutation. I'll see you, bye.

JONATHAN.

*

¹This is the kind of card (in violet ink) I received from the 'Perfect Man':

Dear Fiona!

Puzzled not to hear from you for a while – I do hope you're not unwell, which is code for: are you wearied by my dull company? In any case, could you let me know if you did receive Ramage, as if not I can bully the Post Office.

Ever

PATRICK.

'Ramage' was the author of a rather pious travel book. I had begged the Perfect Man not to lend it to me, but he was never much good at listening. I returned 'Ramage' partially read to the Perfect Man's club with a short note saying that it contained 'too much viewing and too little screwing' for my taste. Since then I have heard nothing.

² Society is made up of swearers and non-swearers; like smokers and non-smokers, they rarely see each other's point of view.

I was brought up in a non-swearing family, preachers in every generation back to the seventeenth century on my mother's side. My grandfather even went to the lengths of buying paperbacks and scribbling out the damns in them. My great-great-uncle, Sam Williams, was the only swearer, but then he *did* join the Army at eleven – he was a big boy – under the assumed name of John Thomas. Apparently I've inherited the exact shape of his thumbs.

I realised as a child that swearing was something I couldn't learn properly at home. I started to compile lists, grading the words from one to ten for shock value. I liked colourful expressions such as 'fuck-a-duck' and 'shit-a-brick'. My best friend's father used 'shit-a-brick' frequently; he even said it when the Bishop of Kensington refused to ordain him.

I used my lists as teaching aids at school – I wanted to make sure all the other little girls had vocabularies as rich as mine. I can still remember the awkward silence at a refined kids' tea-party when someone said: 'Mummy, what's bugger mean? Fiona taught me it today at school.' There's still plenty for me to learn. I didn't latch on to the nicely Freudian 'motherfucker' till I saw a Jack Nicholson film at twenty. More recently, one of my fan letters contained two unknown words – I had to seek a translation from a sixteen-year-old rugby player.

I'm sure there's a book to be written on the psychology of swearing. I once had a lengthy discussion with an American drama student about the relative merits of 'prick' and 'cunt' as abuse. Could they possibly be synonyms in this context? He was convinced the Americans called each other cunts, while the British solely used the word prick. 'Oh no,' I said, 'we call each other both, regularly.'

Of course non-stop swearers – the type that look set for a place in the *Guinness Book of Records* – are a pain. There was one at my art school. He taught Art History. I dropped in once on one of his lectures. 'Monet's a fucking good painter,' he said. 'Fucking good. Look at that fucking beautiful bit of blue in the corner there. Fucking marvellous that, the way it fucking scintillates.' It was a fucking boring lecture – maybe he should have added some buggers for variety.

Swearing's a great relief at times: when you've stubbed your toe, torn your tights, broken your carrier-bag or been let down. It's also extremely useful for getting rid of tiresome men – the sort that follow you at night, or put their hands on your bum in the Tube. I'm inclined to think that kids ought to be taught this by their parents. A timely shout of 'Piss off!' would alert bystanders and also probably ruin the romance of the occasion for the paedophile.

The Elizabethans were more sensible in educating their kids, as lines from Ben Jonson's *Every Man In His Humour* indicate:

> Can it call whore? cry bastard? O then kiss it!
> A witty child! can it swear? the father's darling!
> Give it two plums.

I'd have had a lot of plums from that kind of parent.

I suppose it was the Elizabethans who started getting their oaths slightly wrong: 'Gog' for God, 'Gog's liggings' for God's leggings, whatever those were. There's no reason why you shouldn't invent your own, of course. 'Bugger me black', in one of John Cowper Powys's novels, has a nice feel to it. When I was nine, I enjoyed saying 'Fluck' for weeks before I realised I'd got it wrong.

What I really hate are the saccharin expletives. A friend of mine felt, quite rightly, that she had to have a transfer when she was put into an office with a girl who said 'Fudge!' and 'Sugar!' in a sweet voice all day. I'm getting tired too of the swearing, or rather lack of it, on *Coronation Street*. How can a full-grown, oily motor mechanic like Brian Tilsley be so namby-pamby as to say 'Flaming Nora'? No wonder Gail took up with an Australian – we all know what *they're* like.

Australian Radio was, in fact, broad-minded enough to put out a poem of mine with fucks in it at ten in the morning. When I went on our BBC's *Midweek*, things were very different. There was a last-minute panic discussion to find out what could be read. Fucks, buggery, oral sex, dildoes and wanking were out. In the end they allowed me the childish 'turds' and 'bums'. I *could* have had 'willy', too, but that poem had been used elsewhere. A day or two earlier, I'd offered them a poem called 'Swimming Baths' over the phone. 'It's only got cocks and pubic hair,' I pleaded. The researcher said that was fine. Minutes later she rang back to say it *wasn't* fine, as the cocks were being sucked. (The lines really only describe swimmers' sadistic tales 'of cocks sucked down the deep-end's outlet hole. 'Their owners had the choice – lose it or drown'.)

All BBC precautions proved vain. A French listener misheard my cleanest poem and sent them a translation of it that definitely was kinkier than the original. For the 'lotus position', he heard 'locust position' which doesn't sound like something you do alone. To the impure all things are impure. I should know.

[3] 'Manifesto of a Female Casanova' (*Independent*, 15.10.88), containing extra thoughts on the subjects covered by *Nothing* and *Double Standards*.

'Daddy, what's this pro-mis-cu-ity?' I said, picking it out with difficulty. It had caught my eye on a rather stained page of the *Mirror* which had been wrapped around the cats' giblets. I was just starting to be able to read. I always enjoyed learning new words.

It was a long time before I learnt what it meant in practice. Educational though it certainly is, sex is not something you find on the school curriculum. An Old Etonian once expressed regrets to me on this subject. A party of girls should have been brought in from a neighbouring school, he said. He hinted that he and his co-pupils had become permanently screwed up from lack of being shown how to do it right.

Practical sex lessons of the forced kind could be a problem. Who would partner whom? I remember a spiteful teacher once ordering me to do a project with the school dunce – a girl who got D for everything, burst into tears frequently and, worst of all, had the unlovely habit of scratching piles of white powder off her legs. Luckily I had the guts to refuse flatly this unequal yoking.

A reviewer of my poetry once said that I know as

much about love as a bat does of sunlight. Well, Edward Larissey, I may not know much about love, but I know plenty about lust. I have come to suspect the term 'love' in fact. Voltaire, with whom I share a birthday, after hearing of the tortures his church inflicted on heretics said, '*Ecrasez l'infame!*' I would like to say the same about love. Take a look at the things done in the name of it – the crimes, the sado-masochistic relationships, the lousy destructive marriages. Lust is pretty honest in comparison.

Sex is a constant pleasure. As with anything else, experience in it makes you more skilled. You gain a lot of knowledge about a person, too, while making love. It is one of the quickest ways of getting to know them. Most civilised people are adept at covering their real meanings in conversation, but these are harder to hide when the body's responses are involved.

Apart from the educational aspect, sex has its humorous side. I have a friend who says she 'always laughs at men in bed' because she finds sex so funny. I don't go quite that far. I don't find straight sex particularly ludicrous, but then kinks can be. A person who leads a pure restrained life can have little idea quite how broad the spectrum of male preferences can be. Most of them are fairly harmless, in my opinion, unless they involve cruelty. I tend to keep a straight face then laugh later – I think it's better for my partner's potency. Male approaches are probably the funniest thing of all. Last year, a Sicilian told me that I was lucky to have found him because he was married, and that proved he could not possibly have AIDS. I expect his wife was off saying the same to somebody else.

Religious souls enjoy telling me that, sooner or later, I'll catch some form of VD. (I get the feeling they really want me to.) Well, if I do, at least I'll have the consolation of knowing it wasn't a friend who passed it on to me.

I have avoided conventional nine-to-five jobs all my

life because of a need for adventure. I suppose that I have a lower boredom threshold than most people. One of my friends was stuck at one time in a civil service office where her boss talked non-stop of his ballroom dancing. Such a job sounds to me like the ultimate horror and also a little like some marriages.

My need for freedom and my ambition have both made the serious long-term relationship undesirable. If I had married or lived with someone years ago, I don't think I could have kept on writing till I got published. I would have felt morally bound to waste time on being less of a slut and also to get a sensible job so that I could chip in on the mortgage. As a single person with no ties I was able to devote forty hours a week to writing and live either on the dole or casual jobs as a film extra or teacher. It took me seven years of full-time writing before I could get a book accepted with a major publisher. The money I made from that and the succeeding collection was pitifully low due to scandalous 5% royalty contracts. The literary world is a cruel one – particularly for a poor woman without influence.

We all know that the issue of equal pay is a feminist one. I believe that the right to experiment in sex is one too. I once attended a Mills and Boon lecture – more by accident than design. The whole audience, myself included, was to be groomed for stardom as future romantic novelists. The first step on the road was to be buying and reading a lot of their books. . . . We were told that their heroines were seventeen to twenty-eight, heroes, thirty to forty-five. The heroines weren't allowed to have slept around, the heroes were. All the women in the audience were over twenty-eight and yet they were being asked to subscribe to this excessively old-fashioned fantasy.

In real life, it's certain that a virgin at the upper end of that age bracket, if not excessively religious, would be unattractive and cold-hearted. Is that what we were supposed to admire and empathise with? The lecture resembled hard-sell American evangelism so closely that I felt moved to ask many awkward questions at the end. Mills and Boon heroines couldn't sleep around because 'women who do that are tramps', we had heard. I got up and told the editress in charge that I didn't consider myself a tramp although I'd certainly slept around. She didn't have the nerve to deny the truth of what I was saying – probably because she still saw me as a potential customer cum convert. She just told the manager of the Birmingham Arts Centre afterwards that 'feminists had spoiled her talk.'

I don't think I was being particularly brave declaring my past publicly. After all I've done it all before in poems. (Curiously, readers often choose to disbelieve what I say of myself. I often get asked about the 'personas' I take on and whose stories I tell.) Could I rightly be described as a 'tramp', anyway? I think not. A tramp is a person who has no home, few belongings and who likes travelling. I have a home which is dropping to pieces, thousands of books, a tom cat and four pet seagulls. That's quite a bit of responsibility. Neither am I a nymphomaniac. (Is there any equivalent term invented for men? Labels should be applied to both sexes or not at all.) I'm exceptionally discriminating – I only have it off with good-looking partners. I'm not cheap, I'm free. Life's not a soap opera or a Mills and Boon. Real women – normal healthy women – enjoy sex and take it as one of the best pleasures life can afford.

Some of the old myths and double standards hang on unfortunately. There's the one about slack fannies. Women are supposed to develop these if they have too many men. Now why should that area be different from any other? If you exercise your leg muscles or your arms they're supposed to get tauter and in better shape.

Doctors are always telling us to do things like that. Personally, I'm in favour of exercising everything. If anything stretches a woman it's good old-fashioned, religion-approved, Mills-and-Boon-approved childbirth. The smallest baby's head has to be fatter than any male organ in the *Guinness Book of Records* – that is, if Norris McWhirter stoops to the recording of such things.

People have many hang-ups too about who takes the initiative in a relationship. I can bring myself to ask out a man I know reasonably well already, but I don't think I could walk up to a complete stranger and do it. Would he accept it if I could, anyway? I once made a verbal pass at a man who'd taken me for drinks many times and whinged about how awful his wife was. It seemed clear that the marriage was an open one and, given the fact that he'd compared me to a fluffy white kitten and put his hand on my knee, I thought he might enjoy a little encouragement. I made my pass and Mr Old-fashioned was absolutely horrified. He told me he 'despised me thoroughly' – end of a not-so-beautiful friendship. I was very much surprised in view of the randy image most men seek to give of themselves. Must have been impotent, I comforted myself.

Last year I made three trips to Italy – a part of the world where the men are less cold than my married friend. I was doing research for a travel book. It was not to be Chatto and Windus's answer to Baedeker or the Michelin Guide, but something much more personal. When the holidaying was over, I got down to the serious writing bit. Having gone in for a certain amount of casual sex along my route, I ended up writing a defensive first chapter about the merits of that kind of lifestyle abroad or at home. The chapter was recorded later for a film called *Spinsters*. An all-female company – Steel Bank Films – had decided to include me as an awful contrast to the maiden-aunt type.

In my first chapter, I compared travelling alone to living alone – the two states I choose. My attitude has meant passing most of my life without anyone I could honestly describe as a *regular* boyfriend. It takes more courage to admit that than to own up to sexual experience. People generally see the lack of a man in someone's life as a kind of disability. Coco Chanel once said, 'A woman's nothing if she is not loved.' Judging from what I have read of Chanel's career it was financed and pushed by her lovers. As many others have done, I got by without that kind of help. Perhaps that's why I can see a greater value in a woman's *own* talents and efforts.

When a woman considers herself equal in a relationship she can use as much as she's being used. When the pleasure stops she can walk away. Men have always felt that was open to them. With improved contraception it's open to women too. What's sauce for the goose. . . . I like to believe I'm a sort of female Casanova. I don't think it's a heartless thing to be. Women can do less harm to men than vice versa. Pregancy's out, as is rape. Raping a man may be a nice fantasy, but if you believe Joyce McKinney did it to a Mormon twice her size you have a better imagination than I have.

Articles on stars who've been through several marriages and lots of affairs often describe their love lives as failures. It seems to me that there's another possibility – they knew when to walk out. Becoming famous takes a lot of drive, often the ability to see clearly and go for what you want. If a woman takes that into an affair, then she will drop it once it ceases to have any value in her life. It's the people who put up with lousy relationships who're the real failures. I'd like to hear of the odd marriage counsellor saying, 'For God's sake get rid of so-and-so! You can do a lot better for yourself.'

Women need some kind of emotional bond before

they feel like sex, it's often argued. I haven't noticed. Perhaps I have something missing phrenologically-speaking. Though most of my skull is very well-developed and classical, my bump of reverence seems a little undercut. Probably it is just that men have to feel we need this bond – 'Man's love is of man's life a thing apart, /'Tis woman's whole existence.' In these modern days, when even a test-tubeful of sperm can be a Dad and there are no skills left unique to men, they need this kind of reassurance more and more.

Although I would say that I don't actually *need* a man, I do fancy one from time to time. I consider them as life-enhancers like the Arts or treats like coffee, honey, alcohol and chocolate. While I could live without all these things, life would be poorer. That being said, I also try to rate them as human beings, although some of them make that a little difficult at times.

I'm not unique in my position of loving sex for its own sake. Women tell each other many stories that never get told to the men in their lives. The only thing that makes me unusual is that I've passed some of my stories on to the public to illustrate my personal philosophy. My work is satirical and satire has to be based on truth to work well. Some people who've read my poems think I don't like sex because I have criticised various points of technique. That's as absurd as accusing a literary critic of not liking books.

Sex is an issue which seems to outrage many people – much more than cruelty. I find this hard to understand. It is often found most offensive when a women chooses to speak out about it. I used a couple of harmless little words in a poem about the early definition of sexual roles by the choice of toys. I read this on Radio Wales and there was a mammoth phone in from offended listeners who hadn't noticed the comic's racist jokes just before I went on. Most of them complained about 'a young girl' saying those awful things. While it was nice to be mistaken for a young girl at thirty-three, I felt somewhat surprised – 'piss' and 'prick' are both to be found in the Authorised Version of the Bible. (Prick is of course in a different context – St Paul was kicking against them. Piss though is there, several times, with its usual meaning.)

I expect the *Independent* will receive a lot of letters from Disgusted of Tunbridge Wells (and everywhere else) after this article. I could almost write them beforehand – 'I was a virgin till I married my dear husband at eighteen. We were courting for several years, but never did anything we could be ashamed of in the eyes of God. We have been together for seventy years.' All very nice, my dear, but how do you know he was the best you could have had? And what if you've both been doing it wrong all your lives?

If I ever choose to marry or live with someone it will be because he had more to him than all the dozens of others who couldn't hold me. What higher compliment could I pay a man?

There were, as I foresaw, many letters of reaction to this article; these are three of them:

(Unpublished letter to the editor, 16.10.88.)

Dear Sir,
Has the *Independent* launched a crusade against prudery? Articles on willies and promiscuous women are so boldly presented! Your front page at the weekend only made me sad. Ms Pitt-Kethley is so free she is surely missing that which brings the deepest satisfaction any human being can enjoy – to be truly loved and to truly love.

Yours faithfully

K. MACLENNAN, LONDON

[74]

(Letter – with phone number – to myself, 25.10.88.)

Dear Fiona

I understand that you have had it away with half of Europe – what a pity that I was in the other half!

Yours disgustedly,

TUNBRIDGE WELLS.

(Letter to myself, accompanied by a leaflet on dietary fibre, 15.10.88.)

Ms Fiona Pitt-Kethley,

Thank you very much for your stimulating article in the Weekend *Independent*. It will prevent unemployment in the doctors. It will increase enormously the incidence of heterosexual AIDS, the incidence is already rising and it has always been far more numerous than homosexual AIDS in Africa. Everyone who has been in Africa, and I taught medicine at the medical schools in Kenya and Uganda from 1929 to 1958, knows this. Heterosexual AIDS has almost destroyed the medical services in Africa.

Heterosexual AIDS is now being reported to be rising in Britain. Actually we do not know the true incidence but I read that arrangements are being made to test many thousand men and women, probably they will not know they are being 'tested', to find the true incidence of AIDS. Please don't go and get tested yourself because you may be found to be negative; but even Casanova you may some weeks later be found positive. The blood can develop the change very slowly. *This delay in becoming positive is well recognised by the experts.* So if you carry on and all your numerous clients are negative, they may be slowly becoming positive and vice versa.

I wonder if the Editor of the *Independent* knows about this. It certainly will encourage the spread of AIDS.

You may wonder who I am. I enclose a sheet from the United States' General Mills in 1986 to me and my colleague. I invented the term 'dietary fibre' in 1972 and wrote 3 books on it. I hope you and the Editor take plenty of fibre. It does increase the size of the faeces and cleans the inside.

I suggest that you might benefit and get cleaner inside.

One thing your article did, even to me. I am eighty-four, a widower. The article attracted me; it titillated me into an erection. It could do this to the many thousands who read it. I found it a most stimulating article. It gave me the best erection I have had for many years. You may well have felt that I should phone the local Casanova to come quickly lest I fall into flabbiness.

The editor must be congratulated: it was probably the most read article in the whole newspaper. I am eighty-four years old.

Very sincerely,

. . . (According to his notepaper and a further letter, he is both a doctor and a parson.)

This was my reply, a week later:

Dear . . .
Thank you for your letter.

Let me clear up one or two misconceptions. First, the only 'clients' I have are publishers who pay for my writing. 'I'm not cheap, I'm free.' Secondly, I am already (and always have been) on a high fibre diet. (I can't vouch for the editor of the *Independent* though.)

You say that I would benefit and 'get cleaner inside' from this kind of diet. Well, I have news for you. It has given me a very dirty mind. I credit my eating habits also with the feelings of health and energy that have sent me in search of sex. Perhaps you should think twice before recommending it now you know what effect it has on a woman?

You talk of AIDS. I think most educated people know about the blood taking a long time to become positive. I think they also know about the government recommendations for 'safe sex'. Of course these are not infallible. On the other hand, I think it's fair to argue that some measure of risk is acceptable in life. Just think, next time you go out shopping for your wholemeal bread, muesli and peas, you may be knocked down and rushed to hospital, then have the bad luck to contract AIDS the unpleasurable way – i.e. through a contaminated blood transfusion.

Glad to hear about the erection. I prescribe regular rereadings of my article twice a week.

Yours sincerely,

FIONA PITT-KETHLEY

[4] My poem, *Gents Only*, refers to the following letters:

18.5.82.

Dear Fiona,

How very nice to hear from you! I believe that I had the very real pleasure of meeting you at Hastings (outside the Gents' loos!)

I see that we're both in *Poetry S.E.7.* – will you be attending the reading at the Poetry Society on 1st June?

I enjoyed the enclosed poems, but didn't feel quite able to use them. I hope you'll send more.

Thanks for the subscription.

Good wishes,

HOWARD.

His second letter was an acceptance rather than a rejection. I had figured that he would take a poem once I had subscribed. To test my theory I wrote one called *The Water Official*, definitely not of my usual standard as it only took two minutes to write. (My usual average these days is two weeks' work.) I felt it was a reasonable piece of poetic licence to refer to this acceptance as a rejection, as payment for it was a crumpled £1 postal order.

(Undated.)

> Dear Fiona,
>
> How nice to hear from you. (The last time we met was outside the Gents loo at Hastings – I hope to meet you in more advantageous surroundings some time! I notice that we're both in the next Arts Council anthology: perhaps you'll make it to the usual party?) I shall be pleased to use *Water Official* in *Outposts*. Do have a shot at the 1982 competition.
>
> Good wishes,
>
> HOWARD.

The most amusing fact about these letters is that we met near the bar in a literary festival and never at any time near the Gents! I was not invited to the 'usual party' for the Arts Council anthology. An earlier version of *Gents Only* included the editor's name. I altered this after receiving a long letter from him, begging me to stop persecuting him and saying that he was seriously ill.

My opinions on the 'Gents Only' atmosphere of the literary world are borne out by statistics for publishing and prizes. Some women get through of course, but only about one in eight published poets is a woman. Sometimes rejection slips can be prejudiced too:

(Card to Alan Ross of the London Magazine *from myself, 18.5.88)*

> *Dear Alan Ross,*
> I wasn't going to submit poems to you again. Recently
> though, I mentioned to Hugo Williams your sending me
> a Virago card as a reply. He said it was probably only a
> joke, so I'm trying a few more on you.
>   I hope I've done the right thing?
>   (Reply on back of card:)
>   What's wrong with Virago? You seem to spend your
> time with dreadful men, which gives all your poems a
> disagreeable tone; a pity, because they have possibilities.

[5] Karl – Professor Karl Miller of the *London Review of Books* –
was the earliest major backer of my work. He told me that
editors who disapproved of my outspoken sentiments and bad
language would probably blame my prosody in reviews in
order not to seem moralistic. *Wet Dreams* was a reply to a
poem of Clive James commissioned by the *London Review of
Books* but was published elsewhere as they reckoned I was 'even
more sexist than he was'. I demanded money for the work
done and my relations with the paper, for a time, were a little
strained.

Hugo – Hugo Williams; Blake – Blake Morrison; George –
George MacBeth.

With my contracts on *Sky Ray Lolly* and *Private Parts* I
obtained £200 and £400 advances respectively. The six hundred
quoted was the entire amount of earnings on *Sky Ray Lolly* as
at Spring 1988 when this poem was written. I have mentioned
my 5% royalty in various letters to papers. These are quoted
on the following pages.

'Of course, the Arts Council does grants . . . just three. But
'87 was Carribean Year, so every applicant *had to be* black.'

The grants in 1987 were indeed black only. I am at present

bringing a case – paid for by the Commission for Racial Equality – No: 8718198 in the Westminster County Court, between Helen Fiona Pitt-Kethley and the Arts Council of Great Britain (also known as *Pitt-Kethley versus the Arts Council of Great Britain* for short).

The following is a letter I wrote in reply to these remarks by Jonathan Keates: 'I have been asked to judge another prize . . . and wonder sardonically whether I should pass the invitation to Fiona Pitt-Kethley, whose advertisement in a recent *London Review of Books* announces that she 'wants work giving readings, adjudications etc.' I have a theory that Fiona Pitt-Kethley was devised by the folks at Chatto and Windus in a moment of bibulous exuberance':

Sir, – I would like to assure Jonathan Keates ('Freelance', July 1-7) that Fiona Pitt-Kethley was not devised by the 'folks at Chatto and Windus in a moment of bibulous exuberance'. Frankly, they would not have had the imagination.

I am very grateful to him for his offer of a job judging a novel competition. I shall be happy to accept this and any other forms of adjudication jobs from him or anyone else. He may be interested to know that one of my reasons for advertising for such work in the *London Review of Books* is the extreme stinginess of my publishers. My royalties on the poetry books are a meagre 5 per cent. This is decreased to $\frac{1}{2}$ per cent effectively by the publishers selling off books at less than half price to some booksellers so that they can pay me 5 per cent of the price received rather than the cover price. The royalty department seems to be the sole area of the firm where imagination operates. In view of this kind of treatment, once my travel book *Journeys to the Underworld* is out (in October) I shall be quitting the Chatto stable. I am at present seeking a different major publisher for my next collection.

After one or two other people had remarked on my adverts for work and for an agent in the *London Review of Books*, I wrote to that paper. They entitled the letter 'Gissa Job':

Recently, various writers have expressed surprise at my having advertised for readings or adjudications, and for an agent, in your paper. There are two answers to these people. One is, why not advertise? My own publishers choose not to on the whole, Andrew Motion once told me, because they had found it didn't pay. Apart from the isolated case of Chatto and Windus, advertising seems to work and be a sensible way of selling houses, cars, services – whatever a person has to offer. My other answer is that I need to. I have worked very hard, been very ill-paid, and now have almost no prospects. My adverts were, in a sense, an attempt to find out if there was anyone among your readership courageous enough to lend a helping hand.

On the surface, my current misfortune's odd – people are *supposed* to want and pay highly for wit. I've written witty collections of poetry and have a full-length, extremely unusual, comic travel book, *Journeys to the Underworld*, due out in October. Yet, within the last year, my poems have gradually become much less acceptable. I can now only publish in foreign outlets, women's magazines and the odd small press rag – things outside the British literary scene in other words. Similar problems exist on the readings circuit. I've not been allowed to give a reading from any of my six collections at the Poetry Society. More recently, my last two readings – firm bookings – were axed with extremely vague explanations. Either I've been blacklisted or I'm suffering from a singular dearth of work.

I deal with proofs and correspondence quickly, enjoy publicity, can make an audience laugh, have broadcast often, made TV appearances, been interviewed by many journalists and have lots of fans. So, if there is any editor from a major publishing firm willing to give this model character contracts at a standard rate rather than the unusually low 5 per cent offered by Chatto, he/she will be welcome to Pitt-Kethley's exciting new collection, or a Selected Poems. I would also consider offers from small presses for older work – hundreds of poems and two novellas. I'd like to do more journalism, readings, adjudications – anything of that sort, and I need an agent to represent me, as I have ideas for and have started four novels. I am prepared to work hard – I only ask to be allowed to earn a living.

Poets who may be thinking of emulating my vulgarity and gambling a few pounds on an advert may be interested in the results I've obtained so far – a fee paid in advance for one reading, vague promises of others and tentative calls from a couple of agents. The situation has also had its comic fringe benefits. One caller who wasn't eager to give her name rang to tell me what a wonderful firm Chatto and Windus is! Another, presumably not an 'enterprising agent' or poetry reading organiser, simply breathed – at first. A budgie was chirping merrily in the background. I have visions of the bird betraying him to his wife (or mother?) by saying: 'I've got a nine-inch cock. Do you want to hear me come?' Who wouldn't advertise in a paper that has such a choice and varied readership?

Two replies which were published in the *London Review of Books*:

I have neither a budgie nor a nine-inch cock but I have, as the result of her, apparently, notorious small advertisement in the *LRB*, recently become Fiona Pitt-Kethley's agent. Not only that, but I'm auctioning, repeat auctioning, her third collection of poems, *The Perfect Man*. However good, bad or indifferent a poet posterity may deem Ms Pitt-Kethley, it seems to me that her new collection is hugely entertaining and saleable, and thus publishers should be invited to bid for the rights as they do these days for manuscripts by novelists. Two of the eight publishers to whom I've submitted the manuscript have telephoned to say: 'But you can't auction *poetry!*' Oh yes you can. And now I must stop, as the holiday postcard from St Leonards might say, or I'll miss my flight to the Frankfurt Book Fair to garner offers for *The Perfect Man*.

GILES GORDON.

Ain't it horrible being so neglected! Here I am, another failing poet – ages since I was given a really good publishing – pining for full exposure – just like Fiona P.K. Trouble is, I can't pull down my verbal knickers to the same effect as unabashed Fiona repeatedly has. I've gotta rely on my *poetry*. And perhaps she's exposed her private parts ten times too much. I trust that clits, like even nine-inch dicks, eventually have their day. And their enduring night.

TED BURFORD.

⁶Letters by some of those mentioned in *Pen Friends*:

2.10.85.
Just a word to say how much I enjoyed your poems. I found them at last in a small bookshop in Covent Garden. They don't conform to the preconceived ideas most of us have about poetry – i.e. if they weren't set out in lines they could be mistaken for prose by someone who did not know – but they are great fun to read and full of interesting ideas and feeling, and there's obviously more of yourself in them than there is in most of the conventional poets in their poetry.

Hope you're well and enjoying life – and perhaps we'll meet some time. I'm usually in the Borders, trying to get on with a few translations but emerge every now and again – for instance I'm travelling south this weekend on my way to Barcelona where I am working at a conference on 9 and 10 Oct. I am taking a little three-wheeler car which is rather unstable when there is only one person in it, so there's a lift to Spain and back if you're interested.

I know it's crazy to suggest this as we haven't even met, but people should do crazy things occasionally. So if you're tempted by a few days of sunshine and good French and Spanish food, why not let yourself be tempted?

My boat leaves on Sunday night from Portsmouth – it shouldn't be strikebound as it's French – and goes to Saint Malo from which I hope to drive on Monday to Les Eyzies where the Cromagnon men painted some interesting cave paintings about 35,000 years ago (these unfortunately can't be seen as the caves have been locked up), but there are supposed to be some good reproductions in the local museum) – then on to the Costa Brava on Tuesday.

If you feel like helping to stabilise my car it won't cost you a thing – the trip is paid for anyway – and I can make the detour through Hastings or at least Brighton without difficulty – I'll be leaving from here Saturday afternoon and staying the night somewhere in Yorkshire and the ship only leaves Portsmouth around 9 p.m.

I'll phone from somewhere along my route – probably wherever I stay on Saturday night.

I still do not understand why I'm doing such a weird and irrational thing, but life doesn't last forever and one might as well enjoy it while there's a chance – I hope you won't feel insulted even if you can't accept, but it would be even better if you decide to take a chance on this little trip (we would be back about 13-14 Oct).

Best wishes,

Yours,

ANTHONY.

14.10.86. As at 3.50 p.m. (Sent by registered post with 'articles'.)

Dear Fiona,
Sorry to write again after Monday's missive and no time for reply from you. However, I feel under a compulsion to let you see virtually all the articles, which could be said to be anti-Maggie.

If you think any of the poems and prose articles interesting I would be surprised. Any ideas on splitting up articles and poems to target for publication consideration or corrections on style, content and fact would be greatly appreciated. My best wishes to your mother.

Best wishes,

IAN.

(Undated, early 1988, sent via the BBC with photograph and poem.)

dear fiona
quite involuntarily at first. I have resolved by lateral deduction to visit you. conjecturing the occasion into abstract components and marvelling at the various patterns of development proliferating out of context into compatible orgies of intricate cross fertilization inextricably trivial in their conception yet bearing all the forbidden fruit of an uncastrated imagination. a fascinating hybrid of untold sophistication. loosed into the void of improbability only to be borne again from the nether depths of subconscious oceans on the powerful wings of some bizarre and self indulgent fancy, sustained to all intentional purposes then released again. to become as impersonal as uncut diamonds in a neighbors dustbin, an irrational alignment of such infinitessimal significance that your name would have been lost indefinitely had i not written it down on the spur of the moment after one

of those tedious interviews they have on radio four to fill up space between identical newscasts yawn. i though as i tried to stretch some life back into my brain dead coma . . . finished at last! Now there's a bit of card on my desk bearing the legend, fiona pitt-kethley, radio 4, wednesday afternoon, 3.45, it just so happens that i sign on, on a wednesday, and i got back from cambridge (fifteen miles away) in time to hear that programme.

the very fact that i undertake to visit friends (on my bike) means that i have annihilated the initiative (usually all my own) until i perceive the juxtaposition of two quite different alternations which involve separate flight paths, how can i be in two places at once? i've got to be somewhere or nowhere at all, inertial psychedelic energy conservation a quantum of will power and the notion that it's impossible to make a mistake deliberately, if the novelty wears off 160 miles from home, i'ld be left to my own devices with my own bicycle, the very same random combination of chance and self determination that put me in this unenviable position, it's all to do with the migration of a species threatened with extinction, and the scarcity of suitable territory, and stuff like that if you can accommodate the idea of an oddball, like the one in the picture turning up, ever, your address and phone number might be useful, how about an enlightened scenario designed to enlighten the uninitiated?

feel free to burn all this nonsense, shred it, stick pins in it, whatever you're into

your's spontaneously

john.